From Zero to Eleven Plus: Verbal Rea
Self-tutor study guide for High School Entrance Exams

From Zero to Eleven Plus: Verbal Reasoning introduces verbal reasoning through without testing to time. However, if you have previously practised verbal reasoning questions, it can be used as a test.

The sections are linked in question type, so that the user can get used to a style of question and hence a way of thinking that is required to solve questions quickly and successfully. Also, it should help the identification of the type of question that requires more rehearsal and highlight areas for development, for example, a need to increase the amount of reading and talking in order to expand vocabulary.

It is crucial that after each test the user goes over the answers and works out why errors, if any, have been made as this is a good way to learn and prepare for the following test.

While the tests involve 100 questions to be answered in 50 minutes, it is important to try any unanswered questions and also mark these for learning. As speed is of the essence, leave out questions that you find more challenging, so you don't lose marks on the other questions and then go back to the less obvious questions later.

The tests include twenty six different question types to provide a range of relevant experience and learning. In the answers, tips are provided for all the number-3 questions as these combine mathematical understanding with logic and also for the number-12 questions, as these may require algebraic technique that cannot be self taught.

From Zero to Eleven Plus: Verbal Reasoning is written by experienced practitioners, who have an exemplary record for making a positive difference to exam grades and to gaining a place at top secondary schools. For much less than the cost of one hour's tutoring, it supports outstanding achievement.

Contents

Exercises	2
Test Paper One	7
Test Paper Two	11
Test Paper Three	15
Test Paper Four	19
Answers and tips	23

ISBN: 978-0-9568427-2-5
First Edition – March 2011
Copyright © 2011 by Caroline Brice
Published by Andrew Crisp
3 Godson Road, CR0 4LT, UK
Tel: +44 (0)20 8686 9796
Email: books@zerotoelevenplus.co.uk
Web: www.zerotoelevenplus.co.uk
Editors: Caroline Brice and Amy Brice

From Zero to Eleven Plus: Mathematics and *From Zero to Eleven Plus: English* are also available.
For more information, please visit www.zerotoelevenplus.co.uk

While every effort has been made to ensure the accuracy of the contents of this study-guide, the publisher will accept no responsibility for any errors, or opinion expressed or omissions, or for any loss or damage, consequential or otherwise, suffered as a result of any material here published.

The entire contents of this publication are protected by copyright, full details of which are available from the publisher. All rights reserved. No part of this publication may be reproduced, stored in a retrieval system or transmitted in any form or by any means – electronic, mechanical, photocopying, recording or otherwise – without the prior permission of the copyright owner.

£6.99

EXERCISES

1) Underline one word in the brackets that fits.

   Example: Vicar is to (<u>church</u>, house, bible) as teacher is to (shop, gym, <u>school</u>).

   a) Mother is to child as sheep is to (ewe, lamb, calf).

   b) Hand is to glove as foot is to (sock, ball, kick).

   c) Wallpaper is to (glue, wall, flower) as curtain is to (glass, window, material).

   d) London is to (Wales, England, Scotland) as Paris is to (Spain, America, France).

   e) Flower is to (vase, garden, park) as jam is to (toast, jar, tart).

2) Write the letter that can be moved from the first word so it is still a word, and added to the second word to make a new word.

   Example: steam   buy   (s)

   a) left   right   (   )

   b) stuck   low   (   )

   c) wand   itch   (   )

   d) wart   tin   (   )

   e) mortal   rain   (   )

3) The values of *a, b, c, d* and *e* are either 1, 2, 3, 4 or 5. Work out the value of each letter.

   $a = 2e$ $b - a = e$ $c - d = e$ $2b = c + 1$ $e^2 = e$

   $a = (\ )$ $b = (\ )$ $c = (\ )$ $d = (\ )$ $e = (\ )$

4) Find the middle word by exchanging one letter from the first word to make a new word that can lead to the final word with one more exchange of the letter.

   Example: shore <u>short</u> shirt

   a) shape _____ spare

   b) mane _____ late

   c) glass _____ brass

   d) irate _____ graze

   e) ship _____ chin

5) Insert the letter that ends the sequence.

   A B C D E F G H I J K L M N O P Q R S T U V W X Y Z

   Example: A, C, E, G, I, (K)

   a) A, B, D, E, G, (   )

   b) A, Z, B, Y, C, (   )

   c) A, B, E, F, I, J, (   )

   d) D, C, G, F, (   )

   e) M, K, N, L, O, (   )

6) Underline the odd one out.

   Example: knife, fork, spoon, cup

   a) car, walking, bus, lorry

   b) coat, gloves, hand, hat

   c) February, Wednesday, March, December

   d) reading, dancing, running, swimming

   e) eagle, tuna, mackerel, cod

7) Insert the number that fits the pattern.

   a) 3 (5) 2   4 (10) 6   8 ( ) 15

   b) 12 (5) 7   50 (42) 8   75 ( ) 35

   c) 4 (12) 3   5 (30) 6   9 ( ) 10

   d) 60 (98) 38   16 (33) 17   999 ( ) 2

   e) 10 (5) 2   18 (6) 3   48 ( ) 6

8) Work out which code matches which word and then write the code for the new words given.

mend	pens	sink	germ
5,7,3,8	9,2,10,1	1,2,3,6	4,2,3,5

   a) spend   (, , ,)

   b) pending (, , , , ,)

   c) edge   (, , ,)

   d) snipe   (, , , ,)

   e) edging   (, , , , ,)

9) Underline the word that makes the most sense in each set of brackets.

   Max (watched, saw, surveyed) the room. It was in complete (disarray, disturbance, mess). The safe was (shut, open, wide) and it was empty; the (witch, thief, man) had taken everything. Max was (determined, angry, crazy) to retrieve his papers; in the wrong hands they would cause a lot of trouble.

10) Follow the system of the example to deduce the final word.

    Example: Apple is to grapple as in is to grin

    a) Claw is to law as slit is to _____

    b) Lined is to dine as tamed is to _____

    c) Reward is to ward as because is to _____

    d) Thundering is to thunder as ordering is to _____

    e) Justice is to stick as recline is to _____

11) Complete the following table.

×	4	a)
b)	12	36
c)	d)	144
e)	2	6

12) Martian A has twice as many legs as Martian B, who has twice as many legs as Martian C, who has twice as many legs as Martian D, who has twice as many legs as Martian E. Altogether the Martians have 93 legs. How many legs does each Martian have?

   Martian A has (   ) legs   Martian B has (   ) legs   Martian C has (   ) legs

   Martian D has (   ) legs   Martian E has (   ) legs

13) Find the middle word which adds one letter to the first word and which can have one letter added to make the final word.

   Example: toe <u>tone</u> stone

   a) law _____ claws

   b) lap _____ psalm

   c) cuts _____ crusty

   d) rate _____ create

   e) save _____ leaves

14) Write one letter that completes the first word and begins the other.

   Example: gri (t) race

   a) gri (   ) lace

   b) dra (   ) rin

   c) gentl (   ) clipse

   d) bear (   ) ream

   e) bra (   ) reat

15) Six people sit around a hexagonal table. Who sits where?

   Bella sits next to Anne, who is opposite Sam. Sam must turn to his left to talk to Oliver, who is opposite Bella. Oliver is next to Georgina who is opposite Tom.

16) Find the word that can precede all four words in each line.

   Example: room side ding ridden (bed)

   a) fuse figure front tact (_____)

   b) ship ache line phones (_____)

   c) hale house spire to (_____)

   d) mare fall club gown (_____)

   e) wards side stairs pour (_____)

17) Write the three-letter word, which can be incorporated with the letters in capitals to make a longer word.

   Example: The clothes were WING on the radiator. (ARM – warming)

   a) The CLE was blown out.   (_____)

   b) The POL went to investigate.   (_____)

18) Underline the word that fits the sentence.

   Example: Did you (write, right) the letter?

   a) We (our, hour, are) going to the zoo.

   b) The (site, cite, sight) was badly littered.

19) Underline the word that goes with the first two words.

   Example: sack, blaze (retire, bag, fire)

   a) order, manager (boss, bossy, employer)

   b) gentle, pale (alight, light, slight)

20) In these sentences find and underline the four-letter word that is formed from the end of one word and the beginning of the next.

   Example: The vi<u>car d</u>ecided to raise money for a new clock.

   a) Her mother objected to all the fuss.

   b) His doctor negotiated with the hospital.

21) Organise the capital letters into a word that matches the second word.

   Example: DAHTE disliked   (HATED)

   a) HECOSN selected   (_____)

   b) OMPLECET finish   (_____)

22) Underline the word in brackets that shows the connection between the first two words.

   Example: circle, square (shapes, dance, triangle)

   a) girl, woman (young, female, boy)

   b) pupil, student (academic, school, learner)

23) Write the word that comes from all of the letters but one of the first word to match the definition in the brackets.

   Example: Pears → ears (what you hear with)

   a) THOUGHT → (_____) (even if)

   b) REVEAL → (_____) (go away)

24) a) Two years ago James was twice the age of Sam who is now nine.
       How old is James now?   (_____)

   b) Two years ago Oliver was twice the age of Millie who is now ten.
      How old will Oliver be in four years time?   (_____)

25) Which one letter can precede all three words to make new words?

   Example: bout, mend, long (a)

   a) art, alms, lace   (_____)

   b) win, race, hem   (_____)

26) Write the letter that can be added to the three words to make new words.

   Example: join, mean, meer (t)

   a) cam, at, chat   (_____)

   b) eaves, one, can   (_____)

PAPER ONE

1) Underline one word in the brackets that fits.

   a) eye is to see as nose is to (nosey, snout, smell).

   b) two is to double as three is to (number, treble, third).

   c) drink is to glass as food is to (plate, dinner, shop).

   d) rabbit is to hutch as dog is to (habitat, kennel, park).

   e) day is to light as night is to (day, dark, stars).

2) Write the letter that can be moved from the first word so it is still a word and added to the second word to make a new word.

   a) thing   fan   (   )

   b) plane   dam   (   )

   c) drag   cane   (   )

   d) been   log   (   )

   e) cute   dot   (   )

3) The values of a, b, c, d and e are either 2, 4, 6, 8 or 10. Work out the value of each letter.

   $c^2 = e$ $a \div e = c$ $d - b = e$ $a + c = d$

   $a = (\ \ )$ $b = (\ \ )$ $c = (\ \ )$ $d = (\ \ )$ $e = (\ \ )$

4) Find the middle word by exchanging one letter from the first word to make a new word that can lead to the final word with one more exchange of the letter.

   a) slit _____ slap

   b) peat _____ seam

   c) play _____ plod

   d) break _____ dread

   e) haste _____ pasty

5) Insert the letter that ends the sequence.

   A B C D E F G H I J K L M N O P Q R S T U V W X Y Z

   a) M, N, O, L, K, (   )

   b) A, E, C, G, E, (   )

   c) H, E, F, C, D, (   )

   d) A, K, D, N, G, (   )

   e) A, C, D, F, G, (   )

6) Underline the odd one out.

   a) calf, ewe, lamb, puppy

   b) happy, elated, miserable, ecstatic

   c) orange, green, indigo, banana

   d) wonder, leer, ogle, gape

   e) football, tennis, swimming, cricket

7) Insert the number that fits the pattern.

   a) 20 (32) 12   6 (10) 4   12 (   ) 13

   b) 4 (32) 8   3 (36) 12   11 (   ) 7

   c) 20 (13) 7   98 (16) 82   37 (   ) 19

   d) 8 (2) 4   15 (3) 5   27 (   ) 3

   e) 13 (169) 13   8 (64) 8   12 (   ) 12

8) Work out which code matches which word and then write the code for the new words given.

ruin	gain	rage	turn
5,3,1,2	7,3,5,2	9,6,1,2	5,6,9,8

   a) engrain   (, , , , ,)

   b) engage   (, , , ,)

   c) intrigue (, , , , , ,)

   d) raining   (, , , , ,)

   e) gutter   (, , , ,)

9) Underline the word that makes the most sense in each set of brackets.

   Annie (washed, brushed, cut) her hair in the mirror and then tied it up with a ribbon, her favourite red ribbon. (Perfect!, Terrible!, Disastrous!) she smiled. The mirror was left to reflect on the sunshine-yellow wall as the girl (shut, withdrew, exited) the apartment and counted the (one, fifteen, hundred) steps down to the next floor. She knocked on the door exactly below her door. "Hello Lisa. It's time to go," she (called, answered, questioned), excitedly.

10) Follow the system of the example to deduce the final word.

    a) damaging is to damage as changing is to _____

    b) emotion is to motion as amount is to _____

    c) expansion is to expanding as extension is to _____

    d) wholesome is to hole as bothersome is to _____

    e) homework is to mews as housework is to _____

FROM ZERO TO ELEVEN PLUS: VERBAL REASONING

11) Complete the following table.

+	-3	a)	-8
b) -1	-2		-6
-5	c)		-12
d)	6	e)	

12) Martian A has five times as many legs as Martian E. Martian B has four times as many legs as Martian E. Martian C has three times as many legs as Martian E and Martian D has twice as many legs as Martian E. Altogether the Martians have 60 legs. How many legs does each Martian have?

Martian A has (   ) legs   Martian B has (   ) legs   Martian C has (   ) legs

Martian D has (   ) legs   Martian E has (   ) legs

13) Find the middle word which adds one letter to the first word and which can have one letter added to make the final word.

a) spin _____ spines

b) drip _____ ripped

c) rags _____ grasps

d) lanes _____ glances

e) serve _____ reserve

14) Write one letter that completes the first word and begins the other.

a) signa (   ) eap

b) horne (   ) rain

c) oblig (   ) ndure

d) contrac (   ) ransient

e) tormento (   ) ace

15) There is a parade of six shops. The post office is furthest east. Shop D is between Shop B and Shop C. Shop C is next door but one to the post office. Shop E is closest to Shop B. Write where Shops A, B, C, D and E are situated.

Shop ( )	Shop ( )	Shop ( )	Shop ( )	Shop ( )	Post Office

16) Find the word that can precede all four words in each line.

a) stand   ground   go   dog _____

b) how   thing   body   where _____

c) ever   as   by   after _____

d) gull   food   shell   side _____

e) climax   dote   clockwise   body _____

FROM ZERO TO ELEVEN PLUS: VERBAL REASONING

17) Write the three-letter word, which can be incorporated with the letters in capitals to make a longer word.

   a) The water was BING. (_____)

   b) The BGE was for pedestrians only. (_____)

18) Underline the word that fits the sentence.

   a) He passed (by, buy, bye) in a car.

   b) She sold it (fore, for, four) five pounds.

19) Underline the word that goes with the first two words.

   a) only, fair (sole, just, simply)

   b) performance, prove (explain, show, act)

20) In these sentences find and underline the four-letter word that is formed from the end of one word and the beginning of the next.

   a) The sign at the start of the road caused confusion.

   b) The artist unveiled her new masterpiece.

21) Organise the capital letters into a word that matches the second word.

   a) DIPPER torn (_____)

   b) YACEDED rotten (_____)

22) Underline the word in brackets that shows the connection between the first two words.

   a) mare, stallion (pony, horse, filly)

   b) decrease, lessen (reduce, cheap, total)

23) Write the word that comes from all of the letters but one of the first word to match the definition in the brackets.

   a) FRIEND → (_____) (brute)

   b) MOVED → (_____) (hemispherical roof)

24) a) If, $a+b=7$ $b+c=9$ $2a=6$ what is the total of a and b and c? (_____)

   b) If, $c-a=b$ $4b=20$ $c=3b$ what is the total of a and b and c? (_____)

25) Which one letter can precede all three words to make new words?

   a) hall, melt, wishing (_____)

   b) inch, inner, age (_____)

26) Write the letter that can be added to the three words to make new words.

   a) age, gas, ray (_____)

   b) here, pain, his (_____)

PAPER TWO

1) Underline one word from each set of brackets that connect in a similar way.

   a) one is to (number, odd, first) as two is to (second, couple, more).

   b) green is to (grass, land, apple) as brown is to (dog, bark, animal).

   c) boat is to (water, bath, rowing) as aeroplane is to (airport, sky, people).

   d) book is to (enjoy, read, shelf) as television is to (watch, aerial, screen).

   e) star is to (sky, gas, night) as pebble is to (throw, heavy, beach).

2) Write the letter that can be moved from the first word so it is still a word and added to the second word to make a new word.

   a) slick   hip   ( )

   b) brainy   corn   ( )

   c) simile   ran   ( )

   d) sing   rate   ( )

   e) pant   taped   ( )

3) The values of a, b, c, d and e are either -2, -1, 1, 2 or 3. Work out the value of each letter.

   $c + d = e$ $b - 1 = d$ $a \div e = a$ $2e = a$ $a + d = 0$ $2a - e = c$

   $a = ($ $)$ $b = ($ $)$ $c = ($ $)$ $d = ($ $)$ $e = ($ $)$

4) Find the middle word by exchanging one letter from the first word to make a new word that can lead to the final word with one more exchange of the letter.

   a) chop _____ clip

   b) ruin _____ vein

   c) sine _____ sang

   d) keep _____ deed

   e) elate _____ state

5) Insert the letter that ends the sequence.

   A B C D E F G H I J K L M N O P Q R S T U V W X Y Z

   a) Z, A, Y, B, X, ( )

   b) T, U, W, Z, D, ( )

   c) A, D, C, F, E, ( )

   d) Z, C, F, I, L, ( )

   e) M, O, K, Q, I, ( )

FROM ZERO TO ELEVEN PLUS: VERBAL REASONING

6) Underline the odd one out.

    a) modern, traditional, new, contemporary

    b) lion, dog, cat, rabbit

    c) sprint, stroll, walk, hike

    d) Paris, Belgium, London, Rome

    e) Jupiter, Mars, Neptune, Sun

7) Insert the number that fits the pattern.

    a) 28 (32) 4   16 (31) 15   36 ( ) 12

    b) 5 (5) 1   16 (8) 2   36 ( ) 6

    c) 6 (24) 4   7 (56) 8   9 ( ) 8

    d) 9 (7) 2   42 (29) 13   61 ( ) 18

    e) 4 (48) 12   11 (33) 3   9 ( ) 6

8) Work out which code matches which word and then write the code for the new words given.

    peck   deep   lake   read

    7,9,9,6   3,9,1,7   6,9,8,2   4,1,2,9

    a) peeked (, , , , ,)

    b) deck (, , ,)

    c) leaked (, , , , ,)

    d) ladder (, , , , ,)

    e) clearer (, , , , , ,)

9) Underline the word that makes the most sense in each set of brackets.

The dog (smiled, snarled, meowed) at the menacing beast. The (intimidating, inept, insignificant) creature (exited, advanced, withdrew) towards the dog, leaving the latter in the (fear, room, darkness) of its shadow. The dog was (happy, trapped, blind).

10) Follow the system of the example to deduce the final word.

    a) lower is to slower as cold is to _____

    b) part is to trap as tang is to _____

    c) nets is to tens as felt is to _____

    d) cringe is to ring as sinks is to _____

    e) treasure is to pleasure as tread is to _____

11) Complete the following table.

+		0.7	a)
b)		1.2	2.3
	2.8	c)	4.6
d)		3.8	e)

12) Martian A and B together have the same amount of legs as Martian C. A has double the amount of legs B has. B has double the amount of legs Martian D has. Martian E has four legs more than D. Altogether the Martians have 74 legs. How many legs does each Martian have?

   Martian A has (   ) legs   Martian B has (   ) legs   Martian C has (   ) legs

   Martian D has (   ) legs   Martian E has (   ) legs

13) Find the middle word which adds one letter to the first word and which can have one letter added to make the final word.

   a) oat _____ boast

   b) men _____ women

   c) sole _____ closer

   d) hard _____ harder

   e) dome _____ loomed

14) Write one letter that completes the first word and begins the other.

   a) slo (   ) ith

   b) ba (   ) ension

   c) frictio (   ) ature

   d) laps (   ) lated

   e) to (   ) alace

15) A pizza costs the same as two sandwiches. A pizza and a cola cost £3.40. A sandwich and cola cost £1.90. A chocolate bar costs three times as much as a sweet. A cola costs the same as one chocolate bar and one sweet. How much is each item?

   a) pizza _____

   b) cola _____

   c) sandwich _____

   d) chocolate bar _____

   e) sweet _____

16) Find the word that can precede all four words in each line.

   a) rage   spoken   standing   side   _____

   b) hole   age   hood   made   _____

   c) out   list   mate   ups   _____

   d) free   less   taker   fully   _____

   e) bringing   date   lift   set   _____

17) Write the three-letter word, which can be incorporated with the letters in capitals to make a longer word.

   a) The PL was deserted.   (_____)

   b) Our NEIGHBS are noisy.   (_____)

FROM ZERO TO ELEVEN PLUS: VERBAL REASONING

18) Underline the word that fits the sentence.

   a) It cost (two, too, to) much.

   b) The children had lost (they're, their, there) ball.

19) Underline the word that goes with the first two words.

   a) conquer, controller (master, king, boss)

   b) mission, surgery (office, operation, task)

20) In these sentences find and underline the four-letter word that is formed from the end of one word and the beginning of the next.

   a) Fifty people came to the party.

   b) She happily remembered all their magical moments.

21) Organise the capital letters into a word that matches the second word.

   a) DACEDDRIS rejected (_____)

   b) ENBINGING start (_____)

22) Underline the word in brackets that shows the connection between the first two words.

   a) shirt, skirt (clothes, uniform, dress)

   b) red, blue (yellow, primary, colours)

23) Write the word that comes from all of the letters but one of the first word to match the definition in the brackets.

   a) GRASP → (_____) (intake of breath)

   b) GARDEN → (_____) (annoyance)

24) a) a, b and c are positive integers. If the product of a and b is 5 and the product of a and c is 8 and the product of b and c is 40, what is the value of b? (b=___)

   b) a, b and c are positive integers. If the product of a and b is 10, the product of a and c is 6 and the product of b and c is 15, what is the value of c? (c= ___)

25) Which one letter can precede all three words to make new words?

   a) row, own, rip (_____)

   b) right, east, arm (_____)

26) Write the letter that can be added to the three words to make new words.

   a) boat, mash, lick (_____)

   b) plane, rains, rip (_____)

PAPER THREE

1) Underline one word from each set of brackets that connect in a similar way.

   a) Joke is to (laughter, book, comedian) as sum is to (teacher, fingers, maths).

   b) Wood is to (tree, table, fire) as zoo is to (conservation, animal, lion).

   c) One is to (number, only, odd) as two is to (twins, double, even).

   d) Pen is to (pencil case, eraser, paper) as brush is to (canvas, painting, masterpiece).

   e) Bed is to (bedroom, hotel, sleep) as sofa is to (sitting, people, lounge).

2) Write the letter that can be moved from the first word so it is still a word and added to the second word to make a new word.

   a) about   gain   (   )

   b) strain   tone   (   )

   c) dame   cloths   (   )

   d) moat   cob   (   )

   e) table   sable   (   )

3) The values of a, b, c, d and e are either 1, 9, 10, 81 or 100. Work out the value of each letter.

   $\sqrt{b} = a$ $a - e = c$ $c^2 = d$ $b - a = c + d$

   $a = ($ $)$ $b = ($ $)$ $c = ($ $)$ $d = ($ $)$ $e = ($ $)$

4) Find the middle word by exchanging one letter from the first word to make a new word that can lead to the final word with one more exchange of the letter.

   a) pass _____ pest

   b) crave _____ brake

   c) anger _____ ankle

   d) slack _____ block

   e) hosted _____ pasted

5) Insert the letter that ends the sequence.

   A B C D E F G H I J K L M N O P Q R S T U V W X Y Z

   a) Z, W, T, Q,   (   )

   b) A, G, E, K, I,   (   )

   c) B, C, E, H, L,   (   )

   d) K, I, J, H, I,   (   )

   e) F, C, G, D, H,   (   )

6) Underline the odd one out.

   a) two, five, one, seven

   b) beyond, above, under, later

   c) dress, shirt, trousers, handbag

   d) wasp, fly, spider, moth

   e) stage, dance, sing, act

7) Insert the number that fits the pattern.

   a) 6 (18) 3   4 (20) 5   8 (   ) 2

   b) 9 (3) 3   12 (2) 6   32 (   ) 4

   c) 13 (40) 27   44 (59) 15   18 (   ) 19

   d) 11 (121) 11   14 (196) 14   9 (   ) 9

   e) 72 (8) 9   132 (12) 11   84 (   ) 12

8) Work out which code matches which word and then write the code for the new words given.

       maid   dame   gnat   gene
       1,9,2,9   5,3,4,8   1,2,3,7   8,3,5,9

   a) needed   (, , , , ,)

   b) gaining   (, , , , , ,)

   c) dimmed   (, , , , ,)

   d) tame   (, , ,)

   e) maddening (, , , , , , , ,)

9) Underline the word that makes the most sense in each set of brackets.

   Lennox (fumbled, wrote, drew) with his pen nervously; the exam was about to start. "Okay, you may now turn over your paper," stated the (clear, angry, sulky) voice of the teacher. "You have (ten, forty, four hundred) minutes to write the story," she (screamed, cried, said). "You must (decide, write, choose) from three titles."

10) Follow the system of the example to deduce the final word.

    a) Arm is to harm as elm is to _____

    b) Shelf is to self as shine is to _____

    c) Town is to clown as fear is to _____

    d) Net is to tent as far is to _____

    e) Moss is to loss as mist is to _____

11) Complete the following table.

+	a)		-3
-2		-3	b)
5	c)		2
d)		e)	5

12) Martian A has half as many legs as Martian B has. Martian C has three times as many legs as B has. Martian D has half as many legs as A has. Martian E has as many legs as A, B, C and D altogether. Altogether the five Martians have 190 legs. How many legs does each have?

Martian A has ( ) legs   Martian B has ( ) legs   Martian C has ( ) legs

Martian D has ( ) legs   Martian E has ( ) legs

13) Find the middle word which adds one letter to the first word and which can have one letter added to make the final word.

a) pint _____ sprint

b) rat _____ irate

c) arm _____ charm

d) rigs _____ grinds

e) grain _____ staring

14) Write one letter that completes the first word and begins the other.

a) pen ( ) error

b) thin ( ) ite

c) curtai ( ) abel

d) join ( ) rain

e) arm ( ) elp

15) Jo is half Amy's age. Lisa is two years older than Clare and one year older than Jo. Sofia is three years younger than Lisa. The oldest child is ten. How old is each child?

a) Jo is _____

b) Amy is _____

c) Lisa is _____

d) Clare is _____

e) Sofia is _____

16) Find the word that can precede all four words in each line.

a) side set fore tray _____

b) stand out draw hold _____

c) hem acid eater i _____

d) sign king tray set _____

e) bed fall proof mill _____

17) Write the three-letter word, which can be incorporated with the letters in capitals to make a longer word.

a) Her DITION is said to be serious. (_____)

b) The COUROUS soldier was awarded a medal. (_____)

FROM ZERO TO ELEVEN PLUS: VERBAL REASONING

18) Underline the word that fits the sentence.

   a) If (your, you're, yaw) not finished by six o'clock, please call me.

   b) The bus was (stationery, stationary).

19) Underline the word that goes with the first two words.

   a) expensive, darling (luxurious, posh, dear)

   b) load, group (pack, collection, cargo)

20) In these sentences find and underline the four-letter word that is formed from the end of one word and the beginning of the next.

   a) The group assembled in his dining room each week.

   b) He had always inspired his classes.

21) Organise the capital letters into a word that matches the second word.

   a) FATISSY fulfil   (_____)

   b) VOLEN new   (_____)

22) Underline the word in brackets that shows the connection between the first two words.

   a) one, two (three, half, numbers)

   b) bacon, eggs (breakfast, beans, food)

23) Write the word that comes from all of the letters but one of the first word to match the definition in the brackets.

   a) PLIGHT → (_____) (not heavy)

   b) STRAINS → (_____) (flight of steps)

24) a) Amy has twice as many sweets as Ben, who has ten more sweets than Charlie, who has five sweets. How many more sweets does Amy have than Ben?   (_____)

   b) Luke has three times as many sweets as Josh, who has five times as many sweets as Abbey. If Josh and Abbey have twelve sweets between them, how many sweets does Luke have?   (_____)

25) Which one letter can precede all three words to make new words?

   a) now, new, need   (_____)

   b) raft, link, hilly   (_____)

26) Write the letter that can be added to the three words to make new words.

   a) one, adore, ice   (_____)

   b) all, itch, elm   (_____)

PAPER FOUR

1) Underline one word from each set of brackets that connect in a similar way.

   a) Ewe is to (ram, cow, sheep) as doe is to (stag, horse, turtle).

   b) Man is to (father, beard, football) as woman is to (mother, pink, skirt).

   c) Sea is to (world, fish, deep) as jungle is to (wild, tree, monkeys).

   d) Crisp is to (crunch, packet, ready salted) as cola is to (bottle, fizzy, drink).

   e) Bark is to (tree, dog, brown) as cluck is to (animal, farm, chicken).

2) Write the letter that can be moved from the first word so it is still a word and added to the second word to make a new word.

   a) grain   ware   (   )
   b) lever   bed   (   )
   c) range   pits   (   )
   d) create   ban   (   )
   e) manager   blot   (   )

3) The values of a, b, c, d and e are either 32, 16, 4, 2 or 1. Work out the value of each letter.

   $cb = a$ $e^2 = c$ $ad = a$ $ab = ce$ $b - d = d$ $b^2 = e$

   $a = (\ )$ $b = (\ )$ $c = (\ )$ $d = (\ )$ $e = (\ )$

4) Find the middle word by exchanging one letter from the first word to make a new word that can lead to the final word with one more exchange of the letter.

   a) clasp _____ glass
   b) ruined _____ gained
   c) place _____ elate
   d) shot _____ blot
   e) kettle _____ nestle

5) Insert the letter that ends the sequence.

   A B C D E F G H I J K L M N O P Q R S T U V W X Y Z

   a) N, P, L, R, J,   (   )
   b) A, N, C, P, E,   (   )
   c) S, W, A, E,   (   )
   d) W, D, V, E, U,   (   )
   e) M, N, R, S, W, X, (   )

6) Underline the odd one out.

   a) blonde, brunette, fuchsia, ginger
   b) sniff, shout, bellow, whisper
   c) bandana, earring, necklace, bracelet
   d) multiply, divide, subtract, square
   e) Witchcraft, Christianity, Buddhism, Islam

7) Insert the number that fits the pattern.

   a) 19 (32) 13   7 (33) 26   14 (   ) 27
   b) 7 (63) 9   11 (22) 2   8 (   ) 3
   c) 96 (12) 8   45 (5) 9   132 (   ) 11
   d) 2 (7) 3   3 (10) 5   5 (   ) 7
   e) 14 (2) 7   28 (4) 7   50 (   ) 5

8) Work out which code matches which word and then write the code for the new words given.

road	solo	lone	dent
4,5,8,2	6,5,4,5	7,2,8,3	1,5,9,7

   a) treat   (, , , ,)
   b) saddest (, , , , , ,)
   c) slender (, , , , , ,)
   d) doll   (, , ,)
   e) nodded   (, , , , ,)

9) Underline the word that makes the most sense in each set of brackets.

   Adam (strolled, ran, hopped) home quickly to make sure he wasn't (late, early, slow). His (cousin, friend, parents) would be really angry. Adam had been playing (football, poker, monopoly) with his friends in the park. If only he had taken a (clock, shoe, watch) with him!

10) Follow the system of the example to deduce the final word.

    a) break is to brake as steal is to _____
    b) prince is to pincer as brake is to _____
    c) brass is to rags as blots is to _____
    d) cheap is to peach as steal is to _____
    e) friend is to fiend as grown is to _____

11) Complete the following table.

×	a)		4
12		6	b)
0.2	c)		0.8
d)	e)		12

12) Martian A has three times as many legs as Martian B who has half as many legs as Martian E who has five times as many legs as Martian C who has one third of the legs Martian D has. Altogether the Martians have 76 legs. How many legs does each Martian have?

Martian A has (30) legs   Martian B has (10) legs   Martian C has (4) legs

Martian D has (12) legs   Martian E has (20) legs

13) Find the middle word which adds one letter to the first word and which can have one letter added to make the final word.

   a) beat ___table___ tablet

   b) lapse ___lapsed___ elapsed

   c) pager ___pagers___ grasped

   d) cares ___scared___ creased

   e) grind ___riding___ driving

14) Write one letter that completes the first word and begins the other.

   a) sic (K) eep

   b) radi (O) range

   c) lo (B) eaker

   d) causa (L) eapt

   e) speec (H) acked

15) Distance A to B is twice as far as distance B to C and distance C to D is twice as far as distance A to B but only one eighth of the distance D to E. Distance E to F is three times the distance B to C. Distance A to F is 84 miles. Write down the distance between each point.

   a) A to B ___4___ miles

   b) B to C ___2___ miles

   c) C to D ___8___ miles

   d) D to E ___64___ miles

   e) E to F ___6___ miles

16) Find the word that can precede all four words in each line.

   a) rise   screen   set   burn   ___SUN___

   b) less   table   keeper   sheet   ___TIME___

   c) fume   form   haps   mission   ___PER___

   d) lime   way   marine   heading   ___SUB___

   e) card   man   age   pone   ___POST___

FROM ZERO TO ELEVEN PLUS: VERBAL REASONING

17) Write the three-letter word, which can be incorporated with the letters in capitals to make a longer word.

   a) The WEAR is supposed to get worse. (_____)

   b) The DECOIONS were elaborate. (_____)

18) Underline the word that fits the sentence.

   a) The (whole, hole) class clapped the teacher.

   b) He had put (of, off) writing the letter.

19) Underline the word that goes with the first two words.

   a) fire, bag (blaze, sack, pack)

   b) glue, twig (stick, attach, bind)

20) In these sentences find and underline the four-letter word that is formed from the end of one word and the beginning of the next.

   a) He saw each interviewee was extremely nervous.

   b) The candle shone brightly in the yard.

21) Organise the capital letters into a word that matches the second word.

   a) ERECALP exchange (_____)

   b) READO love (_____)

22) Underline the word in brackets that shows the connection between the first two words.

   a) Amy, Jo (names, young, sisters)

   b) aluminium, iron (magnets, metals, anaemia)

23) Write the word that comes from all of the letters but one of the first word to match the definition in the brackets.

   a) DENY → (_____) (lair)

   b) DREAMT → (_____) (deal)

24) a) Caz is four times the age of Sonny and three times the age of Jordan, who is one year older than Sonny. How old is Caz? (_____)

   b) Maisy is ten times the age of Danny. In four years time, Maisy will be four times the age of Danny, how old is Maisy now? (_____)

25) Which one letter can precede all three words to make new words?

   a) pen, live, at (_____)

   b) mall, now, ink (_____)

26) Write the letter that can be added to the three words to make new words.

   a) dream, our, rusted (_____)

   b) in, right, rat (_____)

ANSWERS

Exercises

1) a) **lamb** b) **sock** c) **wall, window** d) **England, France** e) **vase, jar**
2) a) **f** b) **s** c) **w** d) **w or t** e) **t**
3) a = **2**, b = **3**, c = **5**, d = **4**, e = **1**
4) a) **share** b) **mate** or **lane** c) **grass** d) **grate** e) **shin** or **chip**
5) a) **H** b) **X** c) **M** d) **J** e) **M**
6) a) **walking** b) **hand** c) **Wednesday** d) **reading** e) **eagle**
7) a) **23** b) **40** c) **90** d) **1001** e) **8**
8) a) **5,4,2,3,6** b) **4,2,3,6,7,3,9** c) **2,6,9,2** d) **5,3,7,4,2** e) **2,6,9,7,3,9**
9) a) **surveyed** b) **disarray** c) **open** d) **thief** e) **determined**
10) a) **lit** b) **dame** c) **cause** d) **order** e) **clink**
11) a) **12** b) **3** c) **12** d) **48** e) **0.5**
12) A = **48**, B = **24**, C = **12**, D = **6**, E = **3**
13) a) **claw** or **laws** b) **laps, palm, pals** or **lamp** c) **crust** d) **react** or **crate** e) **slave** or **eaves**
14) a) **p** b) **g** c) **e** d) **d** e) **t** or **g**
15) a) **Tom** b) **Sam** c) **Oliver** d) **Georgina** e) **Anne**
16) a) **con** b) **head** c) **in** d) **night** e) **down**
17) a) **AND** (cleaned) b) **ICE** (police)
18) a) **are** b) **site**
19) a) **boss** b) **light**
20) a) **hero** b) **torn**
21) a) **CHOSEN** b) **COMPLETE**
22) a) **female** b) **learner**
23) a) **THOUGH** b) **LEAVE**
24) a) **16** b) **22**
25) a) **p** b) **t**
26) a) **e** b) **l**

> *Tip for question number 3:*
> Use your knowledge of operations on numbers to spot which letter has the most obvious value. So,
> $e = 1$ as $e^2 = e$ $1^2 = 1$
> Then go to: $a = 2e$ and so on

> *Tip for question number 12:*
> A   B   C   D   E
> 16E 8E   4E   2E   E
> 31E = 93 *So*, E = 3

Paper One

1) a) **smell** b) **treble** c) **plate** d) **kennel** e) **dark**
2) a) **g** b) **e or p** c) **d** d) **n** e) **e**
3) a = **8**, b = **6**, c = **2**, d = **10**, e = **4**
4) a) **slip** or **slat** b) **seat** c) **ploy** d) **bread** e) **paste** or **hasty**
5) a) **P** b) **I** c) **A** d) **Q** e) **I**
6) a) **ewe** b) **miserable** c) **banana** d) **wonder** e) **swimming**
7) a) **25** b) **77** c) **18** d) **9** e) **144**
8) a) **8,2,9,5,6,1,2** b) **8,2,9,6,9,8** c) **1,2,7,5,1,9,3,8** d) **5,6,1,2,1,2,9** e) **9,3,7,7,8,5**
9) a) **brushed** b) **perfect** c) **exited** d) **fifteen** e) **called**
10) a) **change** b) **mount** c) **extending** d) **other** e) **uses**
11) a) **-7** b) **1** c) **-8** d) **9** e) **2**
12) A = **20**, B = **16**, C = **12**, D = **8**, E = **4**
13) a) **spine** or **pines** b) **pride** c) **grass** or **grasp** d) **cleans** or **lances** e) **server** or **severe**
14) a) **l** b) **t** c) **e** d) **t** e) **r**
15) From left to right: **E, B, D, C, A**
16) a) **under** b) **some** c) **where** d) **sea** e) **anti**
17) a) **OIL** (boiling) b) **RID** (bridge)
18) a) **by** b) **for**
19) a) **just** b) **show**

> *Tip for question number 3:*
> Use your knowledge of operations on numbers to spot which letter has the most obvious value. So,
> $c = 2$ and $e = 4$ as $c^2 = e$ and no other number has its squared answer available.
> Then go to: $a \div e = c$

> *Tip for question number 12:*
> A   B   C   D   E
> 5E   4E   3E   2E   E
> 15E = 60 *So*, E = 4

FROM ZERO TO ELEVEN PLUS: VERBAL REASONING

20) a) **gnat** or **hero** b) **stun** or **hear**
21) a) **RIPPED** b) **DECAYED**
22) a) **horse** b) **reduce**
23) a) **FIEND** b) **DOME**
24) a) **twelve** b) **thirty**
25) a) **s** b) **w**
26) a) **p** b) **t**

Paper Two

1) a) **first, second** b) **grass, bark** c) **water, sky** d) **read, watch** e) **sky, beach**
2) a) **s** b) **y** c) **i** d) **g** e) **p**
3) $a = 2, b = -1, c = 3, d = -2, e = 1$
4) a) **chip** b) **rein** c) **sane** or **sing** d) **deep** e) **slate**
5) a) **C** b) **I** c) **H** d) **O** e) **S**
6) a) **traditional** b) **lion** c) **sprint** d) **Belgium** e) **sun**
7) a) **48** b) **6** c) **72** d) **43** e) **54**
8) a) **6,9,9,2,9,7** b) **7,9,8,2** c) **4,9,1,2,9,7** d) **4,1,7,7,9,3** e) **8,4,9,1,3,9,3**
9) a) **snarled** b) **intimidating** c) **advanced** d) **darkness** e) **trapped**
10) a) **scold** b) **gnat** c) **left** d) **ink** e) **plead**
11) a) **1.8** b) **0.5** c) **3.5** d) **3.1** e) **4.9**
12) $A = 20, B = 10, C = 30, D = 5, E = 9$
13) a) **boat** b) **omen** c) **close** or **loser** d) **heard** e) **model**
14) a) **w** b) **t** c) **n** d) **e** e) **p**
15) a) **£3.00** b) **40p** c) **£1.50** d) **30p** e) **10p**
16) a) **out** b) **man** c) **check** d) **care** e) **up**
17) a) **ACE** (place) b) **OUR** (neighbours)
18) a) **too** b) **their**
19) a) **master** b) **operation**
20) a) **type** b) **calm**
21) a) **DISCARDED** b) **BEGINNING**
22) a) **clothes** b) **colours**
23) a) **GASP** b) **ANGER**
24) a) **five** b) **three**
25) a) **g** b) **f**
26) a) **s** b) **t**

Tip for question number 3:
Use your knowledge of operations on numbers to spot which letter has the most obvious value. So, $e = 1$ as $a \div e = a$. Then go to: $2e = a$ and so on.

Tip for question number 12:

A	B	C	D	E
4D	2D	6D	D	D+4

$14D + 4 = 74$
$14D = 70$ So, $D = 5$

Paper Three

1) a) **comedian, teacher** b) **tree, animal** c) **odd, even** d) **paper, canvas** e) **bedroom, lounge**
2) a) **a** b) **r** or **s** c) **e** d) **m** e) **t**
3) $a = 10, b = 100, c = 9, d = 81, e = 1$
4) a) **past** b) **brave** or **creak** c) **angle** or **angel** or **glean** d) **black** e) **posted**
5) a) **N** b) **O** c) **Q** d) **G** e) **E**
6) a) **two** b) **later** c) **handbag** d) **spider** e) **stage**
7) a) **16** b) **8** c) **37** d) **81** e) **7**
8) a) **2,9,9,8,9,8** b) **1,3,4,2,4,2,1** c) **8,4,5,5,9,8** d) **7,3,5,9** e) **5,3,8,8,9,2,4,2,1**
9) a) **fumbled** b) **clear** c) **forty** d) **said** e) **choose**
10) a) **helm** b) **sine** c) **clear** d) **raft** e) **list**
11) a) **-1** b) **-5** c) **4** d) **8** e) **7**

Tip for question number 3:
Use your knowledge of operations on numbers to spot which letter has the most obvious value.
$\sqrt{b} = a$ b must be 81 or 100 and a must be 9 or 10.
$c^2 = d$ c must be 9 or 10 and d must be 81 or 100.
e must be 1. The numbers are therefore defined by $a - e = c$ as a must be 10 and c must be 9 and so on.

12) A = **10**, B = **20**, C = **60**, D = **5**, E = **95**
13) a) **print** or **pints** b) **tear** or **rate** c) **cram** or **harm**
    d) **grins** or **rings** or **grids** e) **grains** or **rating**
14) a) **t** b) **k** c) **l** d) **t** e) **y**
15) a) **five** b) **ten** c) **six** d) **four** e) **three**
16) a) **be** b) **with** c) **ant** d) **as** e) **water**
17) a) **CON** (condition) b) **AGE** (courageous)
18) a) **you're** b) **stationary**
19) a) **dear** b) **pack**
20) a) **pass** b) **sins**
21) a) **SATISFY** b) **NOVEL**
22) a) **numbers** b) **food**
23) a) **LIGHT** b) **STAIRS**
24) a) **fifteen** b) **thirty**
25) a) **k** b) **c**
26) a) **d** b) **h**

> *Tip for question number 12:*
> A   B   C   D   E
> A   2A   6A $\frac{1}{2}$A $9\frac{1}{2}$A
> 19A = 190   So, A = 10

Paper Four

1) a) **ram, stag** b) **father, mother** c) **fish, monkeys** d) **packet, bottle** e) **dog, chicken**
2) a) **a** or **g** b) **l** c) **n** or **e** d) **e** e) **a**
3) a = **32**, b = **2**, c = **16**, d = **1**, e = **4**
4) a) **class** b) **rained** c) **plate** d) **slot** or **lots** or **lost** e) **nettle** or **settle**
5) a) **T** b) **R** c) **I** d) **F** e) **B**
6) a) **fuchsia** b) **sniff** c) **bandana** d) **square** e) **Witchcraft**
7) a) **41** b) **24** c) **12** d) **14** e) **10**
8) a) **3,1,2,9,3** b) **6,9,7,7,2,6,3** c) **6,4,2,8,7,2,1** d) **7,5,4,4** e) **8,5,7,7,2,7**
9) a) **ran** b) **late** c) **parents** d) **football** e) **watch**
10) a) **stale** b) **baker** c) **logs** d) **least** e) **gown**
11) a) **0.5** b) **48** c) **0.1** d) **3** e) **1.5**
12) A = **30**, B = **10**, C = **4**, D = **12**, E = **20**
13) a) **bleat** or **table** b) **please** or **asleep** or **elapse** c) **pagers** or **grapes**
    d) **sacred** or **scared** or **crease** e) **riding**
14) a) **k** b) **o** c) **b** d) **l** e) **h**
15) a) **4** b) **2** c) **8** d) **64** e) **6**
16) a) **sun** b) **time** c) **per** d) **sub** e) **post**
17) a) **THE** (weather) b) **RAT** (decorations)
18) a) **whole** b) **off**
19) a) **sack** b) **stick**
20) a) **chin** or **hint** b) **they**
21) a) **REPLACE** b) **ADORE**
22) a) **names** b) **metals**
23) a) **DEN** b) **TRADE**
24) a) **twelve** b) **twenty**
25) a) **o** b) **s**
26) a) **t** b) **f** or **b**

> *Tip for question number 3:*
> Use your knowledge of operations on numbers to spot which letter has the most obvious value.
> $ad = a$ that is $a \times d = a$ shows that d has a value of 1
> $b - d = d$ shows that $b = 2$
> $b^2 = e$ shows $e = 4$
> $e^2 = c$ shows $c = 16$
> and so on.

> *Tip for question number 12:*
> A   B   C   D   E
> 3B   B   0.4B   1.2B   2B
> 7.6B = 76   So, B = 10

FROM ZERO TO ELEVEN PLUS: VERBAL REASONING